Safe Swallowing
With Dysphagia:

A Puree Cookbook
For Dysphagia-Related Lifestyles

Written By
Sharon Lynn Mercer

Written As A Promise And Labor of Love
Dedicated To
My Mother, Barbara Mercer

DISCLAIMER

The recipes and information contained in this book have not been endorsed by any agency, medical doctor, or medical society. You should consult your doctor or other health care professional prior to using any of the recipes or dietary suggestions in this book. Content in this book is for reference purposes based solely on personal experience, opinion, and reflection. It is not a substitute for advice from a licensed health-care professional. You should not rely solely on this content. Every effort has been made as to the accuracy and correctness of all terminology and information presented. The author is a retired teacher and not a medical professional. Medical information or terminology is not guaranteed as to accuracy or correctness and is not intended as medical advice. It is not intended to diagnose, treat, cure, or prevent any disease or condition. It should not be used in place of talking with your doctor. Always check with your doctor or other professionals in the field when using information presented here or regarding matters discussed in this cookbook.

This book is great! I love how the author uses her own experiences to help families comprehend this very overwhelming condition known as dysphagia. Sharon's personal knowledge helps families to understand the day to day difficulties in providing nourishing home made purée meals.

Lisa Klein, M.S., CCC-SLP
Santa Monica, California

TABLE OF CONTENTS

———— ✱ ————

INTRODUCTION

Safe Swallowing With Dysphagia: *A Puree Cookbook For Dysphagia-Related Lifestyles* was compiled for people facing dysphagia who need basic easy-to-make puree recipes. Although recipes do not indicate calorie counts or have a nutrition breakdown, they do provide a resource to be able to get into the kitchen and prepare dysphagia-appropriate meals. These are the recipes I prepared for my mother. They helped her. I wrote this puree cookbook as a promise to her and a labor of love, in an effort to help others.

Doctors diagnosed my mother's dysphagia! Her swallowing ability was compromised. She had to eat pureed foods because she no longer swallowed properly and risked developing aspiration pneumonia. I had to purchase a food processor, puree her foods, and thicken everything into a nectar, honey, or pudding consistency. It sounded awful and felt impossible.

Eating and drinking became troublesome. Nutritional and caloric intake as well as adequate hydration became an issue. Creativity in the kitchen took center stage. I needed to get inventive, fast. I explored new ways of preparing recipes she liked. Everything needed to be safe to swallow and tasty, in addition to being simple but healthy. Using a food processor, I made pureed foods and drinks that kept her hydrated, were nutritious and had high calorie counts. I needed to make sure my mother enjoyed mealtime, drank enough, ate enough, and that each bite was packed with adequate nutrients. She enjoyed newly concocted puree recipes and began getting stronger. I called her my little medical miracle.

The food processor became a great asset and my best friend. I served small meals frequently throughout the day. Dysphagia stopped being an enemy.

Safe Swallowing With Dysphagia: *A Puree Cookbook For Dysphagia-Related Lifestyles* was written for those diagnosed with dysphagia, a type of swallowing disorder, their family members and caregivers, as well as members of the medical community, in the hope that it will be recommended as a valuable resource by doctors, nurses, speech pathologists, nutritionists, dieticians, and pharmacies.

This cookbook is geared for people who want to find an easy solution to a difficult problem. It is for people needing simple mechanical soft and puree recipes that emphasize nutritional and caloric intake as well as adequate hydration.

Recipes are intentionally unlike those found in typical cookbooks, both by design and by ingredients. Recipes do not adhere to exact measurements, but use dollops, scoops, splashes, handfuls, shakes, swirls, and pinches instead. Lack of precision and approximate cooking times are designed to enhance the flexibility of preparations and to allow for variations in cookware and equipment.

Sections include an introduction and table of contents. There are personal thoughts and a description of what I have learned about the necessary lifestyle changes involving the viscosity or thickness of foods and beverages that I had to make at mealtime when faced with dysphagia. There are basic puree recipes for fruit, breakfast, soups, omelets, sandwiches, vegetables, meat, pasta, fish, and desserts. I've included a shopping list of ingredients required, most of which are found in a typical kitchen. There is a page of approximated conversions for measurements. All recipes are mechanical soft before being pureed and can be adjusted in consistency.

In addition to puree recipes, I've included information about pureed foods and beverages for dysphagia, a listing of online resources for dysphagia, a list of support groups and a list of online resources for conditions that can be affected by dysphagia. Also included is information with lists of dysphagia's possible causes, signs, and symptoms. There is an extensive bibliography of sources that I used in the research and writing of this puree cookbook.

I am a retired teacher and was the primary caregiver for my 90 year old mother whose other age related illness was further complicated by the onset of dysphagia. Her swallowing difficulties created life-threatening problems and sent my creativity from the classroom straight to the kitchen. I collected the recipes I prepared for her and made a promise to her that someday I would publish them, to share them with others who faced similar challenges.

Upon hearing a diagnosis of dysphagia, many people frantically look for guidance to prepare mechanical soft and pureed meals that are safe to swallow and still be tasty, yet simple. I certainly did when my mother was diagnosed. I tried to learn all I could and read everything on the topic I could get my hands on. I listened carefully to the doctors, nurses, speech pathologists, and all of the available medical experts in an effort to try to do the best I could for my mother. These are the recipes for the meals I prepared for her. I tried each before serving to be sure she'd like it. I ate the mechanical soft version. She ate the pureed version. The puree consistency was right for her. She enjoyed these simple recipes collected in **Safe Swallowing With Dysphagia:** *A Puree Cookbook For Dysphagia-Related Lifestyles.*

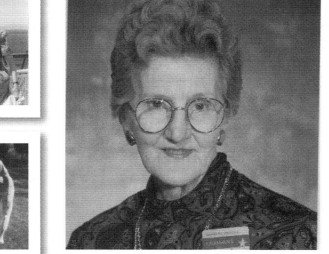

I Made a Promise To My Mother
Barbara Mercer

This Is Some of Her
Biographical Information

Barbara Mercer
March 14, 1916 - December 23, 2006

Safe Swallowing With Dysphagia: *A Puree Cookbook For Dysphagia-Related Lifestyles* is the culmination of my special promise to my mother. After her dysphagia diagnosis, menus consisted of pureed meals, which she enjoyed. We talked about collecting and writing down our recipes to help other people who were facing the same kinds of dysphagia issues. I promised her I was going to write a cookbook of all the meals we pureed.

The photos of my mother displayed in **Safe Swallowing With Dysphagia:** *A Puree Cookbook For Dysphagia-Related Lifestyles* picture her as vivacious, proud, feisty, full-of-life, when nothing could stop her. They show a productive, talented, happy woman, active, gracious, independent, when she was taking care of everything and everyone, when she was still ok. That's who she was; that's how she'd want to be remembered.

Like other daughters, I am convinced my mother was the best ever. She was a devoted wife and mother, loved being a homemaker, and working with the public. She loved her life but it wasn't easy for her.

She struggled all her life, from becoming a ward of the state when she was 2 and placed in Father's Baker's Orphanage at Our Lady of Victory Infant Home in Lackawanna, NY. At 5 she became a foster child picking strawberries on a 40-acre farm in East Eden, NY. She was on her own at 15, doing housework and working as a waitress at Laube's Old Spain next to Shea's Buffalo in downtown Buffalo, then a bride and mother by 30, and a young widow at 51. She retired at 80 after 40 years in sales at Hengerer's Department Store in Amherst, NY, later named Kaufmann's, then Sibley's, now Macy's. Anyone from Buffalo who shopped there knew her. Everyone liked her. She worked hard all her life,

could crack a joke with the best of them, and always had a witty comeback or insightful comment. Always finding time to talk and listen, she was wise and caring, never afraid to speak her mind.

Aromas coming from her kitchen enticed anyone within sniffing distance to join her and enjoy a scrumptious meal. I used to think she was a gourmet cook. In addition to cooking, she loved to sew and all things artistic: singing, dancing, painting, reading, "puttering", the theater, and all genres of music. She dressed in style, loved singing at the piano and had a beautiful voice. My mother was about the handiest woman I knew and didn't bat an eye at recovering a sofa or chair, changing a light socket, replacing a pipe for a plumbing issue, rewiring her electric stove, removing a furnace motor to have it rewired then reinstalling it. She said she'd rather do these things instead of bringing someone in to do something she could do herself. More than once she painted the inside and outside of her two-story home herself, before finally having it sided. There was no stopping her. Not one to watch sit-coms, she enjoyed live TV, watched 60 Minutes and the news, and always kept abreast of current affairs. She was an avid fan of the Buffalo Bills, Perry Como, Elvis, Louis Prima, the Beatles as well as the Four Tops and Temptations; she rarely missed Lawrence Welk, Johnny Carson or later David Letterman. Her home sparkled and her gardens thrived. She loved the outdoors. Always laughing and smiling, she constantly brought joy back into the world. She thanked God everyday for all her blessings and focused on her family. She took great pride in being a wife and making a home for her family. She took great pride in being a mother and wanted her children to have the mother she never did. She'd reminisce about being with Dad when he was stationed in Seattle during the war, and she talked proudly of her two brothers, one who had been in the Battle of the Bulge, the other who had landed in Normandy ten days after the invasion. She enjoyed stimulating conversations and remained "sharp as a tack" until 89 when illness began changing things and dysphagia became a new companion at the table. A vibrant woman with seemingly boundless energy, she had a strong work ethic and uncompromising integrity. She faced adversity head-on with kindness, perseverance, and a positive attitude. Constantly on the go, shopping, cooking, taking care of her family, dancing, having a good time, she was my inspiration, best friend and hero. We'd talk, sing, dance, and laugh for hours on end, sharing our secrets, hopes, and memories.

Throughout her life she was meticulous in all she did, and exuded a dignified refined elegance. Her life exemplified the value of not looking to material things to find happiness. Her gentle heart, sense of humor, and insight gave her the extraordinary ability to make us feel better about everything. Part-time philosopher, she'd say, "Take each day as it comes. There are hills and valleys in life, sunny days and terrible storms. Everyone gets a chance, a share of the good and the bad, of life's joys and sorrows; some get their chance early; some not till very late; everyone gets their share and a turn at life. You have to live each day, make the best of it. You can't sit around worrying or fretting. It doesn't help or change a thing. Enjoy your life. Be kind to everyone. Tell little children how special they are and build them up. Always be patient and grateful for what you have. Get up in the morning, get yourself going, and thank God for another day."

She was a strong woman and never let life get the better of her. Dysphagia was her final challenge. She conquered that too. She amazed me. These puree recipes helped her successfully maneuver through the maze of dysphagia related issues that began to develop. Being discharged from a hospital with a dysphagia diagnosis and only general instructions to buy a blender or food processor so we could puree all meals was very confusing, to say the least. There was so much to learn.

Experimentation became the order of the day. When I had to prepare her puree meals, it was a challenge for me to measure up to her skills in the kitchen. Thankfully, my early exposure to her culinary expertise helped to enhance my creativity. We learned about dysphagia together and prepared puree meals accordingly. These puree recipes reflect my mother's "dysphagia years".

She lived a life of service, as a child on the farm, as a wife and mother, as a sales clerk in the department store. It was her hope that **Safe Swallowing With Dysphagia:** *A Puree Cookbook For Dysphagia-Related Lifestyles* would be of service to others.

She's looking down on this puree dysphagia cookbook that I promised her I'd put together to help others. I know she's smiling, once again healthy, young and beautiful, laughing, singing and dancing, happily reunited with everyone she loved who went before.

My mother will live in my heart and memories forever as the most wonderful one-of-a-kind mother who I'll never forget and forever love. I imagine her applauding **Safe Swallowing With Dysphagia:** *A Puree Cookbook For Dysphagia-Related Lifestyles,* and saying, "Good job, Sharon! I love it!"

From
The First Cry
To
The Cradle
The
Thorns And Roses
Grow

by Barbara Mercer

EVERYDAY
WHEN MY MOTHER
ATE OR DRANK

These behaviors during my mother's meals reflect instructions and guidelines given to me by professionals.

- She was alert, awake, and sitting straight up with her head tilted forward.
- Meals were visually appealing with assorted colors of pureed choices.
- Meals included protein, fruits, vegetables, and a tasty dessert.
- Fresh fruits and vegetables were used whenever possible.
- Thickened beverages accompanied each meal, sometimes with _Pedialyte_.
- _Thick & Easy_, _Resource_, _Boost_ or _Ensure_ drinks were often added to recipes and also accompanied meals to supplement caloric and nutritional intake.
- _Benecalorie_ or _Beneprotein_ was sometimes added to recipes for extra nutrients.
- Small sips followed each bite.
- Alternate foods replaced powdered thickeners whenever possible.
- Small bites made swallowing easier.
- She ate slowly and frequently.
- Meals ended with extra sips of beverages to help her wash everything down.
- I never forced her to eat or drink more than she wanted.
- Stored leftovers maximized her available choices for each meal.
- Mint flavored sponge-like _toothettes_, bought at a surgical supply store, helped clean leftover food particles from her mouth.
- My mother remained sitting for at least an hour after each meal.

MY THOUGHTS
ON
DYSPHAGIA

My thoughts on dysphagia changed since I first heard my mother's diagnosis. I tried to find out all that I could about dysphagia and became an informed caregiver.

Dysphagia affects not only the elderly, but also those suffering from a wide range of illnesses, like Alzheimer's, dementia, stroke, Lou Gehrig's disease, MS, Parkinson's disease, just to name a few. It is devastating news to hear that one's loved one has difficulty with the most basic of needs, eating and swallowing, further complicating an already debilitating illness.

My mother learned new ways of eating and swallowing, and I explored new methods of preparing her meals that did not adhere to exact measurements. I concocted recipes using dollops, scoops, splashes, handfuls, shakes, drizzles, swirls, dashes, and pinches. Lack of precision enhanced the flexibility of my new preparations, all mechanical soft consistency before being pureed.

The thought of pureed foods and thickened liquids was uncomfortable to me in the beginning. In fact, it sounded awful. Perseverance, coupled with trial and error, put a whole new perspective on what seemed intolerable and insurmountable.

New basic recipes emerged for ordinary foods commonly found in our kitchen. Texture changed, not taste, when my mother's food was pureed. Her enjoyment and safe swallowing triumphed over her dysphagia!

SOME OF WHAT I LEARNED ABOUT
VISCOSITY & DYSPHAGIA:
LIFESTYLE MEALTIME CHANGES

Dysphagia or difficulty swallowing is caused by the deterioration of the swallowing mechanisms within the throat. It is directly impacted by the viscosity, consistency, or thickness of foods and beverages and can cause them to "go down the wrong way" when swallowing.

Speech pathologists evaluate individuals who exhibit swallowing difficulty and frequently recommend limiting their diets to pureed foods and thickened beverages. Their recommendation reduces the risk of food "going down the wrong way" into the windpipe or trachea, thereby protecting the lungs from aspiration of foreign substances, which can lead to pneumonia or other problems.

Diets requiring pureed foods and thickened beverages usually are recommended for those with moderate to severe swallowing difficulty and who can't protect their airway very well. Frequent coughing after swallowing is one signature symptom of this.

A fully functional individual has no difficulty swallowing solid foods or thin liquids like coffee, water, clear juice, broth, or whole milk.

With aging or the onset of disease, dysphagia symptoms sometime develop and swallowing safely becomes an issue. The importance of the thickness or viscosity of foods and beverages becomes apparent. As an individual's swallowing capability deteriorates, the need for softer, tender solid foods and thicker beverages increases. Solid food can be difficult to swallow because small pieces can get stuck, and thin liquids travel down the throat much too fast, resulting in fits of coughing. As dysphagia develops, the muscles that control the swallowing mechanisms within the throat do not work properly or fast enough to direct what is being swallowed to travel safely down the correct path.

The rate of movement down the path of the swallowing mechanisms within the throat during swallowing for an individual with progressive dysphagia needs to be slower than that of someone without it.

Doctors frequently order what is known as a "Swallow Evaluation" for someone who shows symptoms such as frequent coughing after eating and drinking or who has recurrent bouts of pneumonia. That is when a speech pathologist may be asked to step in. During a "Swallow Evaluation", a speech pathologist watches an individual eat and drink and frequently places a stethoscope on the neck as swallowing takes place to hear the actual swallowing process. Deciding whether it is necessary to alter the viscosity or thickness level of meals requires listening to the actual swallow in this way by a speech pathologist in order to determine the answer, and each case is different. Follow-up may include a recommendation for a lifestyle mealtime change from a regular diet to a diet consisting of foods that are mechanical soft or pureed and beverages that are thickened.

A mechanical soft diet allows for a variety of textures and consistencies but requires a minimum of chewing. Foods in this category are tender, can be broken apart easily without a knife, and often have a ground texture. Mechanical soft is the first category of softened solid foods for those with swallowing difficulty. Foods in this category are soft and tender and include such things as macaroni and cheese or chopped up Salisbury steak with gravy.

On the other hand, foods in a pureed diet do not allow for a variety of textures, require no chewing, and are always smooth without any separate pieces or chunks that need to be chewed. Chewing can be problematic, so foods that are dry or rough, like raw vegetables, crackers, and breads are off limits on a puree diet. Pureed foods and beverages may have a nectar, honey, or pudding consistency. Liquids such as broth may be added to foods prior to blending to achieve the correct consistency recommended.

Individuals with swallowing problems, who have been put on a puree diet, should always thicken their beverages like water, clear juice, milk, soda pop, and coffee. Solid foods should always be soft and tender.

Food can no longer be quite so solid, and beverages can no longer be thin.

When preparing pureed meals, food must be cooked first until tender and then put into a blender, food processor, or *NutriBullet* to be pulverized. Softening and thinning of solid foods requires adding liquid. When pureeing most solid foods, liquid needs to be added in order to achieve a thinner smooth consistency. Increasing more of a recipe's specific liquid ingredient works better than simply adding water, which will only serve to weaken the flavor. Conversely, pureeing certain fruits and vegetables makes them runny, so thickening agents need to be added to keep them from becoming too thin. Thickening of thin pureed fruits and vegetables as well as thin beverages like juice or coffee becomes necessary to offset the potential hazard of improper swallowing. Effective thickening agents for liquids, such as _Thick & Easy_ powder, are available commercially. There are effective alternatives to the powder that can be used as thickening agents when preparing meals. For example, rice krispies, cornflakes, instant potato flakes, elbow macaroni, or cubed bread slices can be used to thicken such things as gravy or spaghetti sauce.

Foods and beverages prepared for a puree diet fall into 4 viscosity categories of consistency or thickness: thin, nectar, honey, and pudding. There are also three categories for solid foods: regular, mechanical soft, and pudding.

Thin liquids can be sipped with a straw and include such things as broth, water, coffee, beer, and clear juice.

Nectar thick liquids can be drunk out of a cup and include such things as nectar juices, commercial products such as _Boost & Ensure_ or _Resource_ nectar milk, and most vegetable juices such as tomato juice, prune juice, and regular gravy.

The third viscosity category is called honey consistency and includes foods and beverages that pour slowly, that have the consistency of honey. Examples of honey foods and beverages include ordinary honey, tomato sauce, and creamed soups.

The last viscosity category, considered the thickest, is called pudding consistency. Foods and beverages that fall into this category must be eaten with a spoon and resemble the consistency of ordinary pudding or yogurt.

Preparing foods and beverages with the appropriate viscosity or thickness can be challenging. Preparation sometimes is further complicated by the fact that delays from preparation to serving can make a difference and will result in the need to adjust thickness levels. Commercially available thickening products such as _Thick & Easy_ powder may be used, if delays in serving have resulted in the unintended thinning of what has been prepared. Broths or other thin liquids can be added to make foods or beverages thinner, especially if delays in serving have resulted in the unintended thickening of what has been prepared.

Additional complications can involve the limited ability to consume enough. Inadequate hydration or ineffective caloric intake can be offset by using supplemental nutrient-enhanced products such as _Boost, Ensure, Thick& Easy_ or _Resource_ nectar milk, or _Pedialyte_, as well as calorie and protein powders like _Benecalorie_ or _Beneprotein_.

Speech pathologists work closely with nutritionists and dieticians all of whom are good resources for anyone who wishes to further understand how to best approach the lifestyle changes required during meals due to dysphagia-related symptoms. These professionals can offer suggestions for a wide array of methods and solutions for dealing with this frequently overwhelming challenge. They are available to answer questions and concerns, to increase one's confidence that nutritional needs during mealtime are being met, and to ensure the successful tackling of dysphagia.

Dysphagia is certainly a challenge, but it isn't an impossible challenge.

ONLINE RESOURCES
FOR DYSPHAGIA:

Dysphagia Research Society: www.dysphagiaresearch.org

American Speech-Language-Hearing Association: www.asha.org

Hormel Health Labs: www.hormelheathlabs.com

Nestle Health Science: www.nestlehealthscience.com

Memorial Sloan Kettering Cancer Center: www.mskcc.org

The Dysphagia Institute at Froedtert & the Medical College of Wisconsin
www.froedtert.com and www.froedtert.com/gastroenterology

University of Pittsburgh Schools of the Health Sciences; University of Pittsburgh Medical Center; UPMC Swallowing Disorders Center: www.upmc.com

The Stroke Association: www.strokeassociation.org

The Voice and Swallowing Institute; New York Eye and Ear Infirmary of Mount Sinai
www.nyee.edu

Roswell Park Cancer Institute: www.roswell park.org

Mayo Clinic: www.mayoclinic.org

National Foundation of Swallowing Disorders: www.swallowingdisorderfoundation.com

ONLINE
DYSPHAGIA SUPPORT GROUPS

www.inspire.com/conditions/dysphagia
www.swallowingdisorderfoundation.com
www.endo-education.com/dysphagia-support

ONLINE RESOURCES
FOR CONDITIONS AFFECTED
BY DYSPHAGIA

Alzheimer's Disease
www.alz.org

Dementia
www.dementiasociety.org

Stroke or Brain Injury
www.biausa.org Brain Injury
Association of America

Lou Gehrig's Disease/ ALS
Association
www.alsa.org

Multiple Sclerosis MS
www.nationalmssociety.org
www.mymsaa.org

Parkinson's Disease
www.apdaparkinson.org
www.pdf.org

Diabetes
www.diabetes.org

Cancer
www.cancer.org
www.cancercenter.com

Huntington's Disease
www.hdsa.org

Amyotrophic Lateral Sclerosis ALS
www.alsa.org

Cerebral Palsy
www.cerebralpalsy.org
www.marchofdimes.org

SWALLOWING DIFFICULTIES SHOULD NOT BE IGNORED.
DYSPHAGIA CAN BE LIFE-THREATENING.

Causes of Dysphagia May Include:
Gerd
Head or Spinal Cord trauma
Cancer of the throat or esophagus
Inflammation or swelling of the throat
Neurologic disease
Stroke
Multiple Sclerosis
Multiple Dystrophy
Parkinson's Disease
Dementia
Stricture in throat or esophagus
Side Effect of Chemotherapy or Radiation
Cerebral Palsy
Sjogren's Syndrome
Degenerative disease
Amyotrophic Lateral Sclerosis
(ALS or Lou Gehrig's Disease)
Alzheimer's Disease
Weakened throat muscles

**Signs or Symptoms of Dysphagia
May Include:**
Feeling like food is stuck in the throat
Sensation of a lump in the throat
Excessive coughing after eating
Difficulty swallowing or chewing
Recurrent pneumonia
Frequent need to clear the throat
Sensation of being out of breath when eating
Drooling when eating
Gurgly sounding voice
Feeling the need to reposition the head
when swallowing

People With Dysphagia May Experience:
Recurrent pneumonia
Aspiration of food
Dehydration
Malnutrition
Coughing fits
Anxiety

Medical Professionals May Say:
Muscle weakness in the throat
may lead to dysphagia.

Speech Pathologists perform swallow
evaluations to assess dysphagia.

Speech Pathologists may recommend
thickened fluids and pureed foods.

Tilting the head forward when
eating may be helpful.

Eating or drinking small amounts
slowly may be helpful.

Learning a different way to
eat may be helpful.

Other treatments for dysphagia include
exercises for throat muscles, surgery,
medication changes.

Unresolved dysphagia may
require a feeding tube

IMPORTANT WORK IS BEING DONE BY:

1. **The American Speech Language Hearing Association**
www.asha.org

2. **The Dysphagia Research Society**
www.dysphagiaresearch.org

3. **The National Foundation of Swallowing Disorders**
www.swallowingdisorderfoundation.com

4. **The Dysphagia Institute at Froedtert & the Medical College of Wisconsin**
www.froedtert.com
www.froedert.com/gastroenterology

5. **University of Pittsburgh Schools of the Health Sciences; University of Pittsburgh Medical Center; UPMC Swallowing Disorders Center**
www.upmc.com

6. **The Voice and Swallowing Institute; New York Eye and Ear Infirmary of Mount Sinai**
www.nyee.edu

7. **Roswell Park Cancer Institute**
www.roswellpark.org

8. **Memorial Sloan Kettering Cancer Center**
www.mskcc.org

For All Recipes in the Book

Cooking Times May Vary

ADJUST THE CONSISTENCY FOR ANY RECIPE:

- Add liquid or thickener and blend to the consistency you need.
- Adding liquids will give a thinner result. Adding thickening agents will give a firmer result.
- Use a food processor, blender, or _NutriBullet_.
- Differences in cookware and equipment will affect recipe preparation.
- For a puree diet, blend until smooth.
- For a mechanical soft diet, blend until a minimum of chewing is necessary and tender food is easy to separate without using a knife.
- Add 1 scoop of _Benecalorie_ or _Beneprotein_ for extra nutrients.

APPROXIMATED CONVERSIONS
FOR
MEASUREMENTS

Dollop	¼ cup
Scoop	1 heaping tablespoon
Splash	1 tablespoon
Handful	¼ cup
Shake	1 teaspoon
Swirl	¾ teaspoon
Pinch	½ teaspoon
Drizzle	½ teaspoon
Dash	¼ teaspoon
Container	8 ounces
Can	15 ounces
Bag	16 ounces
Box	16 ounces

FRUIT

STRAWBERRY MILKSHAKE

CRANBERRY ORANGE

1 bag frozen strawberries
1 can strawberry <u>Boost</u> or <u>Ensure</u>
<u>Thick & Easy</u> or <u>Resource</u> powdered thickener

1 can cranberry sauce
1 can Mandarin oranges
3 scoops orange marmalade
3 scoops applesauce
1 container orange yogurt
7-8 crumbled graham crackers
3 pinches brown sugar
3 pinches nutmeg
3 pinches sugar

Steps:

Puree strawberries in a food processor. Add <u>Boost</u> or <u>Ensure</u> and combine together. Add powdered thickener to obtain desired consistency

Pureed fresh strawberries are even better

Add variety of pureed fruits to any <u>Boost</u>, <u>Ensure</u>, or <u>Thick & Easy</u> or <u>Resource</u> beverage to make a delicious smoothie.

Try adding <u>Pedialyte</u> to beverages

Steps:

Combine cranberry sauce, oranges, marmalade, applesauce, and yogurt in a food processor. Puree together. Add graham crackers to obtain desired consistency. Add nutmeg and sugar to taste.

PEACHES, PEARS, APPLESAUCE, OR FRUIT COCKTAIL

1 can of peaches, pears, applesauce, or fruit cocktail
1 flavored yogurt

Steps:

Combine 1 can of fruit and 1 container of flavored yogurt. Puree in a food processor. Add <u>Thick & Easy</u> or <u>Resource</u> thickening powder to obtain desired consistency.

PINEAPPLE COTTAGE CHEESE WITH MINT MANDARIN ORANGE

1 can Mandarin oranges
1 container pineapple cottage cheese
1 container orange yogurt
1 drizzle mint jelly

Steps:

Puree Mandarin oranges in a food processor. Add cottage cheese and yogurt with mint jelly. Puree all ingredients together.

(Note: This makes a fabulous side dish with pureed diced deli ham.)

AMBROSIA

1 container peach, orange, or pineapple yogurt
1 can drained crushed pineapple
1 can drained sliced peaches
1 can drained mandarin oranges
1 scoop marshmallow cream
1 scoop coconut cream concentrate
5 graham crackers

Steps:

Combine chosen yogurt flavor with crushed pineapple, drained peaches, and mandarin ranges. Mix in marshmallow and coconut cream concentrate. Puree all ingredients in a food processor. Add graham crackers as a thickening agent to obtain desired consistency.

CUCUMBER, TOMATO, FRESH STRAWBERRIES, MANGO, PAPAYA, OR CANTALOUPE

1 cucumber
1 tomato
1 small container of fresh strawberries
1 mango
1 papaya
1 cantaloupe
Thick & Easy or Resource thickening powder
1 cottage cheese or 1 flavored yogurt

Steps:

Peel and dice individual fruits. Combine cottage cheese or flavored yogurt with one of the following fruits to have a fabulous side dish: cucumber, tomato, strawberries, mango, papaya, or cantaloupe. Puree. Add Thick & Easy or Resource thickening powder to obtain desired consistency.

CANTALOUPE, CREAM CHEESE, AND CHERRY PIE FILLING

1 cantaloupe
1 container cherry yogurt
1 can cherry pie filling
1 package softened cream cheese
1 splash lemon juice

Steps:

Scoop out cantaloupe. Cut into small cubes. Combine cantaloupe with cherry yogurt, cherry pie filling, and softened cream cheese. Add a splash of lemon juice. Puree in a food processor.

BREAKFAST

CEREAL

1 <u>Thick & Easy</u> or <u>Resource</u> nectar milk
Cereal: Cornflakes, cheerios, rice crispies,
oatmeal, or cream of rice
Pureed fruit or flavored yogurt
Maple syrup

Steps:

Combine and puree nectar milk and cereal. Add pureed fruit or flavored yogurt with maple syrup to taste.

FRENCH TOAST

2 eggs
1 <u>Thick & Easy</u> or <u>Resource</u> nectar milk
2 slices potato bread

Steps:

Beat 2 eggs with nectar milk. Cube 2 slices of potato bread into small pieces. Combine eggs, milk, and cubed potato bread. Microwave 5-8 minutes, until slightly puffy. Add maple syrup and puree.

EGGS BENEDICT

½ can deviled ham
3 eggs
1 handful shredded cheddar cheese
1 container lemon yogurt
7 Ritz crackers

Steps:

Hard-boil 3 eggs. Dice the hard-boiled eggs. Combine eggs with deviled ham, cheddar cheese, and lemon yogurt. Crumble 7 Ritz crackers and combine with egg mixture. Soak until soft. Heat in microwave 2-3 minutes until bubbly. Puree.

HUMMUS

1 can garbanzo beans
1 small container sour cream
1 container plain yogurt
4 slices softened American cheese

Steps:

Combine all ingredients in a food processor and puree.

SOUP

GAZPACHO SOUP

1 can diced tomatoes
1 cucumber
1 handful baby carrots
1 dollop onion dip
1 dollop vegetable dip
1 splash vinegar
1 splash lemon juice
2 eggs
1 small scoop sugar
1 pinch basil
1 pinch garlic
1 pinch parsley
1 can low salt tomato juice

Steps:

Hard-boil both eggs. Dice each of the following: eggs, cucumber. Boil and mash baby carrots. Place diced ingredients and mashed carrots into a food processor and puree. Combine pureed mixture with 1 can of diced tomatoes, onion dip, vegetable dip, vinegar, lemon juice, sugar, basil, garlic, and parsley. Puree a second time. Add tomato juice and puree a third time until desired consistency is reached.

CREAM OF CORN SOUP

1 can creamed corn
1 can diced tomato
1 dollop onion dip
1 handful baby carrots
1 roasted red pepper
1 handful instant potato flakes
1 handful shredded Swiss cheese
1 dollop vegetable dip

Steps:

Dice roasted red pepper Place diced red pepper into a food processor and puree. . Boil and mash baby carrots. Combine pureed mixture with mashed baby carrots, 1 can of diced tomatoes and 1 can creamed corn. Add shredded Swiss cheese, instant potato flakes, onion dip, and vegetable dip. Puree a second time. Microwave 10-12 minutes. Puree a third time.

SPLIT PEA SOUP
LENTIL SOUP
VEGETABLE SOUP

1 can split pea soup
1 can lentil soup
1 can vegetable soup

Steps:

Cook canned split pea, lentil, or vegetable soup. Thicken with instant potato flakes, cooked cream of rice cereal, cooked elbow macaroni, cubed bread slices, or crumbled crackers. Puree to desired consistency.

Any canned soup can be thickened this way.

PUMPKIN SOUP

1 can pumpkin pie filling
1 Thick & Easy or Resource nectar milk
1 tablespoon cinnamon
1 tablespoon nutmeg
5 cloves
1 tablespoon maple syrup
1 scoop cream of rice cereal

Steps:

Combine all ingredients. Microwave 3-4 minutes until bubbly. Remove cloves. Add and microwave needed additional cream of rice cereal to achieve desired consistency.

OMELETS

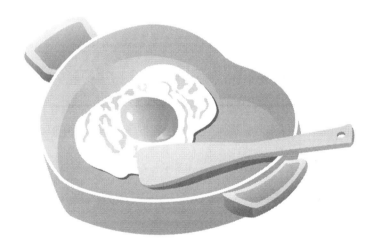

CHEESE OMELET

2 eggs
1 Thick & Easy or Resource nectar milk
1 slice American cheese

Steps:

Beat eggs until fluffy. Crumble cheese. Add nectar milk. Microwave 5-8 minutes until puffy.

ORANGE OMELET WITH RASPBERRY

2 eggs
1 container orange yogurt
2 slices potato bread
1 drizzle raspberry jelly

Steps:

Beat eggs until fluffy. Add eggs to the yogurt and beat together. Cube potato bread. Soak cubed bread in the egg and yogurt mixture. Microwave 5-8 minutes until puffy. Puree and drizzle with raspberry jelly.

Try using lemon yogurt or whole wheat or rye bread as an alternative.

SPINACH TOMATO OMELET

2 eggs
1 Thick & Easy or Resource nectar milk
1 cup frozen chopped spinach
1 handful Parmesan cheese
1 can diced tomatoes
1 sprinkle nutmeg
3 slices American cheese

Steps:

Beat eggs until fluffy. Add nectar milk. Microwave chopped spinach in a covered dish 3-4 minutes until soft. Crumble American cheese. Add cooked spinach, Parmesan cheese, American cheese, and diced tomatoes to egg mixture. Microwave 10-12 minutes until puffy. Puree to desired consistency.

TURKEY LEMON OMELET

3 eggs
1 Thick & Easy or Resource nectar milk
1 container lemon yogurt
4 slices potato bread
3 slices baked roast deli turkey
3 slices American cheese

Steps:

Beat eggs until fluffy. Add eggs to nectar milk and yogurt and beat together. Crumble cheese and add to egg mixture. Cube potato bread. Chop the deli turkey. Soak cubed bread and turkey in the egg, milk, cheese, and yogurt mixture. Microwave 10-12 minutes until bubbly. Puree.

Try using cream cheese or whole wheat or rye bread as an alternative.

VEGETABLE GARBANZO OMELET

4 eggs
1 Thick & Easy or Resource nectar milk
1 can French green beans
½ bag frozen chopped spinach
1 can garbanzo beans
1 package softened cream cheese
1 dollop onion dip
1 can diced tomatoes
4 slices potato bread
1 drizzle mayonnaise or Miracle Whip

Steps:

Beat eggs. Add eggs to nectar milk and cream cheese. Beat together until fluffy. Add onion dip. Puree together. Puree green beans and garbanzo beans. Microwave frozen spinach in a covered dish for 3-4 minutes until soft. Combine eggs, onion dip, bean mixture, Cube potato bread. Mix and puree potato bread cubes with diced tomatoes and spinach. Combine all pureed ingredients together. Microwave 10-12 minutes until

CHEESY VEG MUSHROOM OMELET

3 eggs
1 Thick & Easy or Resource nectar milk
1 can mixed vegetables
1 dollop onion dip
2 handfuls mushrooms
1 can diced tomato
1 summer squash
2 handfuls Parmesan cheese

Steps:

Beat eggs and nectar milk until fluffly. Drain mixed vegetables. Add egg mixture to mixed vegetables, diced tomatoes and onion dip. Dice mushrooms. Saute mushrooms until golden brown and puree. Cut summer squash in half. Microwave for 6-8 minutes until soft inside. Scoop out the squash and add pureed mushrooms. Combine egg and vegetable mixture with squash, onion dip, and mushroom mixture. Add Parmesan cheese. Microwave 10-12 minutes until puffy. Add drizzles of vegetable dip and Parmesan cheese. Place in a food processor and puree until smooth.

SANDWICHES

CHICKEN, HAM, OR TURKEY SANDWICH

3 slices deli chicken
2 slices potato bread
1 handful frozen broccoli florets
1 handful baby carrots
1 can diced tomatoes
1 swirl sweet pickle relish
1 tablespoon mayonnaise or Miracle Whip

Steps:

Dice into cubes 2 slices of potato bread. Dice chicken. Boil and mash baby carrots and broccoli florets. Combine potato bread cubes, diced chicken, mashed baby carrots, and broccoli with 1 can of diced tomatoes. Mix together in a food processor with sweet pickle relish and mayonnaise or Miracle Whip. Puree thoroughly until smooth.

CHEESE AND TOMATO SANDWICH

2 diced tomatoes
2 handfuls shredded American cheese
½ can red kidney beans
2 slices potato bread
1 drizzle vegetable dip

Steps:

Dice 2 whole tomatoes. Cube 2 slices of potato bread. Add tomatoes and cubed potato bread to red kidney beans and shredded American cheese. Drizzle with vegetable dip. Mix together and microwave 3-4 minutes until bubbly. Puree.

PEANUT BUTTER & JELLY SANDWICH

2 slices bread
peanut butter & jelly
1 _Thick & Easy_ or _Resource_ nectar milk

Steps:

Make a regular peanut butter & jelly sandwich. Cube the sandwich and mix together with the nectar milk. Puree by adding _Thick & Easy_ or _Resource_ nectar milk to the mixture until desired consistency is reached.

Any sandwich can be made this way.

REUBEN SANDWICH

½ can sauerkraut
1 can corned beef
1 bag shredded Swiss cheese
1 container plain yogurt
1 dollop Thousand Island dressing
1 drizzle mustard
4 slices seedless rye or pumpernickel

Steps:

Cube 4 slices bread. Puree the corned beef with sauerkraut in its own juices. Combine Swiss cheese, yogurt, Thousand Island dressing, and mustard. Soak cubed bread in cheese and yogurt mixture. Mix together with the pureed corned beef and sauerkraut. Microwave 6-10 minutes until bubbly. Puree.

SLOPPY JOE

1 pound ground beef
1 dollop onion dip
1 handful instant potato flakes
½ jar Heinz chicken gravy
1 handful brown sugar
1 can diced tomatoes
1 can mixed vegetables
3 slices potato bread
1 dash paprika

Steps:

Saute' ground beef until brown. Cube 5 slices of potato bread. Drain mixed vegetables and combine with diced tomatoes and onion dip. Add gravy, brown sugar, paprika, and pepper. Soak potato cubes in vegetable mixture. Mix in the browned ground beef and instant potato flakes. Microwave the mixture 10-12 minutes until bubbly. Place in a food processor and puree thoroughly until a smooth consistency is reached.

VEGETABLES

GREEN BEANS/ DICED TOMATOES

1 can green beans
1 can diced tomatoes
1 container plain yogurt

Steps:

Puree green beans or diced tomatoes as a side dish. Combine with plain yogurt.

Puree any canned vegetable with plain yogurt as a side dish.

MINTED HONEY APPLE AND CARROTS

1 bag baby carrots
1 can apple pie filling
1 dollop honey
1 dollop mint jelly

Steps:

Boil and mash baby carrots. Combine mashed carrots with apple pie filling, honey, and mint jelly. Microwave 4-5 minutes until bubbly. Puree thoroughly until smooth consistency.

FANCY CREAMED SPINACH

1 bag frozen chopped spinach
1 can mushroom soup
½ can red kidney beans
1 container plain yogurt
1 small jar pimento
1 dollop onion dip
1 sprinkle nutmeg
2 handfuls Parmesan cheese
6 Ritz crackers

Steps:

Microwave frozen spinach in a covered dish 3-4 minutes until soft. Puree spinach until smooth. Crush crackers and set aside. Puree kidney beans and pimentos. Mix pureed beans and pimentos with spinach. Add mushroom soup, plain yogurt, Parmesan cheese, and onion dip. Stir in nutmeg and crushed crackers. Microwave 7-8 minutes until bubbly. Puree until smooth.

CREAMED BABY PEAS & ONIONS WITH MARMALADE

1 package frozen baby peas
1 package creamed baby onions
1 drizzle onion dip
1 scoop mint jelly
1 scoop orange marmalade

Steps:

Microwave baby peas and onions 5-6 minutes in a covered dish until soft. Puree peas and onions. Combine with onion dip, mint jelly, orange marmalade. Microwave 3-4 minutes until bubbly. Puree until smooth consistency is reached.

CREAMY MACARONI & CHEESE, BROCCOLI AND GARBANZO BEANS

1 box macaroni & cheese
1 bag frozen chopped broccoli
1 can garbanzo beans
1 Thick & Easy or Resource nectar milk

Steps:

Prepare macaroni & cheese until tender according to box instructions. Boil and mash frozen broccoli. Combine macaroni & cheese, broccoli, garbanzo beans. Puree until smooth. Add nectar milk to obtain desired consistency.

ASPARAGUS AND ROASTED RED PEPPER WITH POTATO

1 can asparagus spears
1 roasted red pepper, large
5 slices deli ham
1 handful instant potato flakes
1 container lemon or orange yogurt
1 dash nutmeg
1 pat of butter
1 Thick & Easy or Resource nectar milk

Steps:

Dice roasted red pepper and deli ham. Combine with asparagus spear and puree thoroughly until smooth.. Mix pureed mixture together with yogurt and potato flakes. Stir in the nectar milk and butter. Microwave 6-8 minutes until bubbly. Puree.

CHEESY CAULIFLOWER, GARBANZO, AND ROASTED RED PEPPER

1 bag frozen cauliflower
2 slices American cheese
1 can garbanzo beans
1 container cottage cheese
1 roasted red pepper, large

Steps:

Cook frozen cauliflower until soft. Drain. Crumble cheese on top. Mix cauliflower and cheese with garbanzo beans, cottage cheese, and roasted red pepper. Puree thoroughly until a smooth consistency is reached. Microwave 5-7 minutes until bubbly.

SLICED BEETS VINAIGRETTE

1 can sliced beets
2 splashes vinaigrette dressing
2 pinches brown sugar

Steps:

Combine beets, brown sugar, and vinaigrette dressing. Microwave 2-3 minutes. Puree.

SWEET POTATO

1 sweet potato
1 pat butter
2 drizzles maple syrup

Steps:

Microwave sweet potato 4-5 minutes until soft. Scoop out inside. Add maple syrup and butter. Puree

SUMMER SQUASH

1 summer squash
1 dollop onion dip
1 pat butter

Steps:

Microwave squash until soft. Scoop out inside. Combine squash and onion dip. Add maple syrup and butter. Puree until a smooth consistency is reached.

BRUSSEL SPROUTS, TOMATOES, AND DEVILED HAM

1 bag frozen brussel sprouts
1 can diced tomatoes
1 can deviled ham

Steps:

Boil and mash brussel sprouts. Combine with diced tomatoes and deviled ham. Microwave 3-4 minutes until piping hot. Place in a food processor and puree thoroughly until smooth.

VEGETABLE MEDLEY

1 dollop onion dip
2 handfuls potato flakes
1 yellow squash
1 roasted red pepper
1 zucchini
1 handful baby carrots
1 handful mushrooms
1 bag frozen broccoli florets
1 bag frozen cauliflower
1 can diced tomatoes
1 can red kidney beans
1 scoop sugar
3 handfuls Parmesan cheese

Steps:

Boil and mash baby carrots, cauliflower, and broccoli florets. Add onion dip. Peel squash and microwave until soft. Scoop out inside and add to the mashed carrots, broccoli and onion dip. Dice roasted red pepper and puree until smooth. Saute' mushrooms until brown. Puree sautéed mushrooms. Combine sautéed mushrooms with mashed carrots, broccoli, and cauliflower. Puree mashed broccoli and carrots with the broccoli and cauliflower. Puree together until smooth. Combine kidney beans and tomatoes. Puree together. Combine all pureed ingredients. Add sugar and Parmesan cheese to the mixture. Microwave 10-12 minutes until bubbly. Puree until smooth.

VEGETABLE LOAF

1 bag baby carrots
1 bag frozen broccoli florets.
1 yellow squash
1 green squash
1 dollop onion dip
4 eggs
1 package cream cheese
1 scoop sugar
1 Thick & Easy or Resource nectar milk
6 American cheese slices
1 handful seasoned bread crumbs

Steps:

Beat eggs and nectar milk until fluffly. Mix egg mixture with cream cheese, onion dip, and sugar. Boil and mash squash, broccoli florets, and baby carrots. Combine egg and cheese mixture with mashed vegetables. Stir in crumbled American cheese, nectar milk, and bread crumbs. Microwave 10-15 minutes until bubbly. Puree thoroughly until a smooth consistency is reached.

MEATS

CHERRY PINEAPPLE HAM WITH SPINACH

1 pound deli ham
1 can crushed pineapple
3 sprinkles brown sugar
1 dollop cherry pie filling
1 handful instant potatoes
1 bag frozen chopped spinach

Steps:

Microwave frozen spinach in a covered dish 3-4 minutes until soft. Dice deli ham. Puree spinach and ham together. Puree pineapple, cherry pie filling, and sugar together. Mix both pureed mixtures with instant potatoes. Microwave 7-8 minutes until bubbly. Puree.

FRUITY HAM WITH BROWN RICE AND COTTAGE CHEESE

1 pound deli ham
½ box brown rice
2 pinches brown sugar
1 can fruit cocktail
1 container pineapple cottage cheese

Steps:

Prepare brown rice according to instructions on the box. Puree the rice using some of the fruit cocktail juices. Chill. Dice deli ham. Add diced ham and brown sugar to fruit cocktail and cottage cheese. Puree together. Serve ham and fruit mixture over rice.

BEEF STEW

1 pound ground beef
1 bag baby carrots
1 bag frozen broccoli florets
1 dollop onion dip
7 small red potatoes
2 dashes brown sugar
1 jar Heinz brown gravy
1 can vanilla <u>Boost</u> or <u>Ensure</u>

Steps:

Boil and mash baby carrots and broccoli florets. Brown ground beef. Add brown gravy and mashed carrots and broccoli to the beef. Puree beef with the mashed carrots and broccoli. Stir in onion dip. Dice red potatoes. Saute until brown and mash browned potatoes. Add mashed potatoes to the beef, mashed carrots and broccoli. Puree together. Add brown gravy and vanilla <u>Boost</u> or <u>Ensure</u>. Bring to a boil and stir thoroughly.

Use 2 scoops <u>Orrington Farms</u> low-salt beef soup base, as a substitute for Heinz gravy.

GROUND BEEF AND PINEAPPLE COTTAGE CHEESE WITH TOMATO

½ ground beef
1 dollop onion dip
1 jar Heinz beef gravy
1 container pineapple cottage cheese
2 tomatoes
1 dash brown sugar
4 slices raisin bread

Steps:

Brown ground beef. Cube raisin bread and soak in beef gravy. Dice 2 tomatoes. Combine browned ground beef, onion dip, gravy with raisin bread, and diced tomatoes. Stir in pineapple cottage cheese. Microwave 5-6 minute until bubbly. Place in a food processor and puree thoroughly until smooth.

Use 2 scoops <u>Orrington Farms</u> low-salt beef soup base, as a substitute for Heinz gravy.

MEATLOAF

1 pound ground beef
2 eggs
1 dollop onion dip
1 dash brown sugar
1 bag frozen chopped spinach
1 squirt ketchup
1 can diced tomatoes
1 jar Heinz beef gravy
1 can Garbanzo beans

4 handfuls Parmesan cheese
3 handful instant potato flakes
10 Ritz crackers
5 handfuls cereal: cornflakes, rice krispies, cheerios, or shredded wheat
½ loaf of potato bread

Steps:

Beat eggs until fluffy. Brown ground beef. Microwave frozen spinach in a covered dish 3-4 minutes until soft. Boil and mash baby carrots. Combine mashed carrots with eggs and onion dip. Mix well. Add browned ground beef, spinach, and diced tomatoes. Puree together until smooth. Combine Garbanzo beans, gravy, potato flakes, crackers, and cereal and puree together until smooth. Combine beef and bean mixtures. Mix thoroughly. Add brown sugar, Parmesan cheese, and squirt of ketchup. Microwave 10-15 minutes until bubbly. Puree.

Adding cinnamon makes a delicious twist.

Use 2 scoops <u>Orrington Farms</u> low-salt beef soup base, as a substitute for Heinz gravy.

VANILLA COCONUT CHICKEN TENDERS WITH STRAWBERRIES

1 pound chicken tenders
1 container vanilla yogurt
5 slices potato bread
4 shakes Mrs. Dash seasoning
1 jar Heinz chicken gravy.
1 can vanilla Boost or Ensure
3 scoops coconut cream concentrate
1 bag frozen strawberries

Steps:

Turn potato bread slices into crumbs using the food processor. Season crumbs with Mrs. Dash seasoning. Let strawberries thaw. Puree strawberries and set aside. Coat chicken tenders with vanilla yogurt. Roll each of the chicken tenders in potato bread crumbs. Bake chicken at 400 for about 30-40 minutes. Combine cooked breaded chicken tenders with gravy. Puree chicken and gravy thoroughly until a smooth consistency. Mix together with vanilla yogurt and Boost or Ensure. Combine coconut cream concentrate and thawed strawberries. Puree coconut and strawberries together until smooth and add to chicken mixture. Mix thoroughly. Microwave 4-5 minutes until bubbly. Puree.

Use 2 scoops Orrington Farms low-salt chicken soup base, as a substitute for Heinz gravy.

LASAGNA

1 package precooked lasagna sheets
1 pound ground beef
1 jar Heinz beef gravy
1 egg
1 bag frozen chopped spinach
1 container Ricotta cheese
1 can red kidney beans
1 jar tomato sauce
1 package Mozzarella cheese
1 scoop Parmesan cheese

Steps:

Purchase precooked lasagna sheets. Brown ground beef. Add gravy to ground beef. Puree beef in the gravy until smooth. Beat egg until it is fluffy. Mix beaten egg with Ricotta cheese and kidney beans. Microwave spinach in a covered dish 3-4 minutes until soft. Puree egg, cheese, beans, and spinach together until smooth. In baking pan, begin to layer precooked lasagna sheets, ground beef and gravy, tomato sauce, spinach, Ricotta cheese and kidney bean mixture, Mozzarella cheese. Bake at 350 for 1 hour. Puree thoroughly in a food processor until smooth.

Substitute low fat cottage cheese for Ricotta cheese. Use 2 scoops <u>Orrington Farms</u> low-salt chicken soup base, as a substitute for Heinz gravy.

GROUND BEEF EGG PUDDING

1 handful ground beef
1 dollop onion dip
1 jar Heinz beef gravy
2 eggs
1 pinch brown sugar
1 vanilla <u>Boost</u> or <u>Ensure</u>
2 slices potato bread

Steps:

Saute ground beef until brown. Add small amount of beef gravy and puree until smooth. Beat 2 eggs with either <u>Boost</u> or <u>Ensure</u> and brown sugar. Cube bread slices and soak in egg mixture and remaining gravy. Combine onion dip, pureed beef, egg mixture, and soaked bread slices. Microwave 10-12 minutes until puffy. Puree.

Use 2 scoops <u>Orrington Farms</u> low-salt beef soup base, as a substitute for Heinz gravy.

DEVILED HAM, EGGS, AND GREEN BEANS

½ can deviled ham
1 can French style green beans
3 eggs
1 scoop sweet relish
6 slices potato bread
1 drizzle mayonnaise or Miracle Whip

Steps:

Hard-boil eggs and chop. Cube 6 slices of bread. Combine deviled ham, green beans, eggs, relish, and mayonnaise or Miracle Whip. Microwave 4-6 minutes to heat thoroughly. Puree.

GROUND BEEF, CUBE STEAK, OR PORK CHOPS

1 pound ground beef, cube steak, or boneless pork chops
1 egg
I dollop onion dip
4 slices whole wheat bread
3 handfuls mushrooms
1 jar Heinz beef or pork gravy
1 can vanilla Boost or Ensure

Steps:

Beat egg until fluffy. Dip beef, cube steak, or pork chop in egg, then brown.
Dice and sauté mushrooms until brown. Puree sautéed mushrooms. Add onion dip with a little gravy, approximately half, and puree with beef, or cube steak, or pork chop until meat is a smooth texture. Cube bread and soak in remaining gravy. Place all ingredients into a baking dish. Cover mixture with Boost or Ensure. Bake at 350 for 2 hours, until bubbly and tender. Puree until a smooth consistency.

Use 2 scoops Orrington Farms low-salt beef or pork soup base, as a substitute for Heinz gravy.

PORK CHOPS WITH PEACHES

1 egg
4 boneless pork chops
½ jar Heinz pork gravy
1 can peach pie filling
½ can peach juice
1 pinch brown sugar
1 can vanilla _Boost_ or _Ensure_

Steps:

Beat egg until fluffy. Dip pork chop in egg, then brown. Combine pork chops with a little gravy, approximately half, and puree until a smooth texture. Place in baking dish with remaining gravy, pie filling, brown sugar, juice, and _Boost_ or _Ensure_. Bake at 350 for 2 hours, until bubbly and tender. Puree thoroughly until a smooth texture.

Use 2 scoops _Orrington Farms_ low-salt pork soup base, as a substitute for Heinz gravy.

CURRY PORK CHOPS WITH SPINACH AND MUSHROOM

1 egg
4 boneless pork chops
½ jar Heinz pork gravy
1 can strawberry _Boost_ or _Ensure_
1 bag frozen chopped spinach
1 can mushroom soup
2 pinches mild curry powder
6 slices potato bread

Steps:

Beat egg until fluffy. Dip pork chop in egg, then brown. Combine pork chop with a little gravy, approximately half, and puree until a smooth texture. Place in baking dish with remaining pork gravy. Add mushroom soup and curry powder. Microwave frozen spinach in a covered dish 3-4 minutes until soft. Cube bread. Soak cubed bread in _Boost_ or _Ensure_. Add spinach and bread mixture to the pork chops. Bake at 350 for 2 hours, until bubbly and tender. Puree thoroughly until a smooth consistency.

Use 2 scoops _Orrington Farms_ low-salt pork soup base, as a substitute for Heinz gravy.

PORK CHOPS WITH CRANBERRY

1 egg
4 boneless pork chops
½ jar Heinz pork gravy
1 dollop onion dip
½ bag frozen broccoli florets
1 handful baby carrots
1 can cranberry sauce
3 splashes of cranberry juice

2 dollops orange marmalade
2 dollops peach pie filling
1 can strawberry Boost or Ensure
1 pinch brown sugar
2 dashes nutmeg
2 dashes cinnamon
5 cloves

Steps:

Beat egg until fluffy. Dip pork chop in egg, then brown. Combine pork chop with a little gravy, approximately half, and puree until a smooth texture. Boil and mash broccoli and baby carrots. Mix in the onion dip. Combine pork chops, carrots and broccoli. Add cranberry juice, cranberry sauce, orange marmalade, peach pie filling. Place in a baking dish with remaining pork gravy and Boost or Ensure. Add brown sugar, nutmeg, and cinnamon. Bake at 350 for 2 hours, until bubbly and tender. Puree thoroughly until smooth consistency.

Use 2 scoops Orrington Farms low-salt pork soup base, as a substitute for Heinz gravy.

PORK CHOPS WITH APPLE, OATS, AND HONEY

1 egg
4 boneless pork chops
½ jar Heinz pork gravy
1 can strawberry Boost or Ensure
2 packages instant oatmeal
1 can apple pie filling
3 dollops honey

Steps:

Beat egg until fluffy. Dip pork chop in egg, then brown. Combine pork chop with a little gravy, approximately half, and puree until a smooth texture. Microwave both packages instant oatmeal according to instructions on the box. Stir in apple pie filling and honey to the cooked oatmeal. Combine pureed pork chops and oatmeal mixture in a baking dish with gravy and Boost or Ensure. Bake at 350 for 2 hours, until bubbly and tender. Puree thoroughly until smooth.

Use 2 scoops Orrington Farms low-salt pork soup base, as a substitute for Heinz gravy.

STUFFED PORK CHOPS

1 egg
4 boneless pork chops
½ jar Heinz pork gravy
1 can strawberry Boost or Ensure
1 bag frozen broccoli florets
1 box pork stuffing mix
1 can mixed vegetables
1 can red kidney beans
1 small jar applesauce
1 dollop honey

Steps:

Beat egg until fluffy. Dip pork chop in egg, then brown. Combine pork chop with a little gravy, approximately half, and puree until a smooth texture. Boil and mash broccoli florets. Combine the stuffing mix with mixed vegetables, kidney beans, and applesauce. Puree stuffing mix with the vegetables until smooth. Stir in honey, gravy and nectar milk. Combine honey, gravy, and milk with pureed browned pork chops and pureed stuffing broccoli and pureed vegetable mixtures in a baking dish. Mix well. Bake at 350 for 2 hours, until bubbly and tender. Puree thoroughly until smooth.

Use 2 scoops Orrington Farms low-salt pork soup base, as a substitute for Heinz gravy.

ITALIAN SWEET SAUSAGE SQUARES

1 pound Italian sweet sausage
1 drizzle olive oil
2 eggs
2 dollops onion dip
1 summer squash
1 bag frozen broccoli florets
4 handfuls Ritz crackers
4 handfuls Parmesan cheese
3 slices American cheese
1 can tomato juice

Steps:

Place sausage in frying pan. Cover with water and boil to cook thoroughly. Drain. Add olive oil to the boiled drained sausage and thoroughly brown. Add onion dip and puree sausage until a smooth texture. Microwave a summer squash 5-6 minutes until soft. Scoop out the inside of the squash and add to pureed sausage and onion dip mixture. Boil and mash broccoli. Crumble Ritz crackers and Parmesan cheese together. Beat eggs until fluffy. Soak crackers, mashed broccoli, and cheese in the beaten eggs. Combine all ingredients in a baking dish. Mix thoroughly. Cover with American cheese. Bake at 350 for 1 hours. Cut into squares. Puree individual squares in tomato juice as needed until a smooth consistency. Heat to serve.

ITALIAN SWEET SAUSAGE AND APPLES

1 pound Italian sweet sausage
1 onion
1 drizzle olive oil
1 can apple pie filling
1 handful Parmesan cheese
3 slices American cheese

Steps:

Place sausage in frying pan. Cover with water and boil to cook thoroughly. Drain. Add olive oil to the boiled drained sausage and thoroughly brown. Add onion dip and puree sausage until a smooth texture. Combine with pie filling, Parmesan cheese, and American cheese. Microwave 10-15 minutes until bubbly. Puree thoroughly until smooth.

SAUSAGE, SPINACH AND CHEESE

CHICKEN, STUFFING, BABY PEAS, AND GRAVY

1 pound Italian sweet sausage
1 onion
1 drizzle olive oil
1 can strawberry Boost or Ensure
1 bag frozen chopped spinach
1 can diced tomatoes
1 handful Parmesan cheese

1 pre-baked chicken
1 box chicken stuffing mix
1 jar Heinz chicken gravy
1 Thick & Easy or Resource nectar milk
1 can mixed vegetables
1 can baby peas

Steps:

Steps:

Place sausage in frying pan. Cover with water and boil to cook thoroughly. Drain. Add olive oil to the boiled drained sausage and thoroughly brown. Add onion dip and puree sausage until a smooth texture. Microwave chopped spinach in a covered dish 3-4 minutes until soft. Combine pureed sausage and cooked spinach. Add tomatoes, Parmesan cheese, Boost or Ensure, and American cheese. Mix well. Microwave 6-8 minutes, until bubbly. Puree thoroughly until smooth.

Purchase pre-baked chicken. Separate from the bone and remove skin. Dice the chicken and combine with stuffing mix, chicken gravy, nectar milk. Add drained mixed vegetables and baby peas. Microwave 6-8 minutes. Puree thoroughly until smooth

Use 2 scoops Orrington Farms low-salt chicken soup base, as a substitute for Heinz gravy.

LEMON CHICKEN, CRABMEAT, ASPARAGUS WITH MASHED POTATOES

1 pre-baked chicken
1 jar Heinz chicken gravy
1 package imitation crabmeat
1 can asparagus spears
2 containers lemon yogurt
3 handfuls instant potato flakes
3 dashes dill

Steps:

Purchase pre-baked chicken. Separate from the bone and remove skin. Dice the chicken and combine with gravy, instant potatoes, yogurt, and dill. Puree together. Dice the crabmeat and the asparagus spears and puree together. Add pureed crabmeat and asparagus to the pureed chicken mixture. Mix well. Microwave 6-8 minutes until bubbly. Puree.

Use 2 scoops Orrington Farms low-salt chicken soup base, as a substitute for Heinz gravy.

CHICKEN CELERY BAKE

1 pound chicken tenders or breast
½ jar Heinz chicken gravy
2 dollops onions dip
1 can cream of celery soup
1 Thick & Easy or Resource nectar milk
1 cup water

Steps:

Dice chicken. Add onion dip. Puree together. Combine pureed chicken and onion dip with gravy, cream of celery soup, nectar milk, and water. Bake at 350 for 2 hours until bubbly. Puree thoroughly until a smooth texture.

Use 2 scoops Orrington Farms low-salt chicken soup base, as a substitute for Heinz gravy.

CHICKEN GARBANZO BAKE

1 pre-baked chicken
1 jar Heinz chicken gravy
1 can cream of celery soup
1 Thick & Easy or Resource nectar milk
1 bag frozen chopped spinach
3 handfuls instant mashed potato flakes
1 can garbanzo beans
1 can diced tomatoes
1 dollop onion dip
6 slices American cheese
3 handfuls Parmesan cheese

Steps:

Purchase pre-baked chicken. Separate from the bone and remove skin. Dice the chicken and combine with gravy, instant potatoes, nectar milk, and cream of celery soup. Stir in onion dip. Puree together until smooth. Microwave frozen spinach in a covered dish 3-4 minutes until soft. Combine pureed chicken mixture with spinach. Add diced tomatoes, garbanzo beans, American cheese and Parmesan cheese. Microwave 8-10 minutes until bubbly. Puree thoroughly until smooth.

Use 2 scoops Orrington Farms low-salt chicken soup base, as a substitute for Heinz gravy.

CHICKEN, BROCCOLI, TOMATO, PARMESAN STEW

1 pre-baked chicken
1 Thick & Easy or Resource nectar milk
1 jar Heinz chicken gravy
1 bag frozen broccoli florets
1 can mixed vegetables
1 can diced tomatoes
2 handfuls Parmesan cheese

Steps:

Purchase pre-baked chicken. Separate from the bone and remove skin. Dice the chicken and combine with gravy and nectar milk. Puree chicken and gravy. Boil and mash broccoli. Combine pureed chicken and gravy with mashed broccoli. Add mixed vegetables, diced tomatoes, and Parmesan cheese. Microwave 8-10 minutes until bubbly. Puree thoroughly until smooth.

Use 2 scoops Orrington Farms low-salt chicken soup base, as a substitute for Heinz gravy.

AVOCADO CHICKEN

1 pre-baked chicken
1 avocado
1 dollop onion dip
2 handfuls of mushrooms
½ can diced tomatoes
3 splashes lemon juice
1 pinch sugar
½ jar Heinz chicken gravy

Steps:

Purchase pre-baked chicken. Separate from the bone and remove skin. Dice the chicken and combine with gravy, diced tomatoes and onion dip. Puree together. Dice mushrooms and sauté until brown. Puree sautéed mushrooms. Peel and dice avocado. Combine pureed sautéed mushrooms, and avocado with chicken, gravy, onion dip, and tomatoes. Add lemon juice and sugar. Microwave 8-10 minutes, until bubbly. Puree thoroughly until smooth.

Use 2 scoops Orrington Farms low-salt chicken soup base, as a substitute for Heinz gravy.

CHICKEN, PEACHES, AND BROWN RICE

1 pre-baked chicken
½ jar Heinz chicken gravy
1 can peach pie filling
1 can peach juice
1 container peach yogurt
½ box brown rice

Steps:

Purchase pre-baked chicken. Separate from the bone and remove skin. Dice the chicken and combine with gravy. Add peach pie filling, juice, and yogurt. Puree together. Prepare rice according to box instructions. Add cooked rice to pureed chicken mixture. Microwave 8-10 minutes, until bubbly. Puree thoroughly until a smooth consistency.

Use 2 scoops Orrington Farms low-salt chicken soup base, as a substitute for Heinz gravy.

TURKEY, BROCCOLI, CHEESE

4 slices baked deli turkey
4 slices American cheese
1 bag frozen broccoli florets
½ _Thick & Easy_ or _Resource_ nectar milk

Steps:

Dice slices of turkey and cheese. Boil and mash broccoli florets. Combine turkey, cheese and broccoli. Add nectar milk. Microwave 3 minutes, until bubbly. Puree thoroughly until smooth consistency.

TURKEY, GINGER, AND ORANGE

½ pound baked deli turkey
1 can mandarin oranges
5 shakes of ginger
1 container orange yogurt
1 splash orange juice

Steps:

Dice the turkey. Combine with oranges, ginger, yogurt, and juice. Microwave 3-4 minutes. Puree thoroughly until smooth consistency.

PASTA

MACARONI TUNA SALAD

½ box elbow macaroni
1 can Albacore solid white tuna
4 eggs
1 can of baby peas
½ *Thick & Easy* or *Resource* nectar milk
1 dollop sweet pickle relish
1 drizzle mayonnaise or Miracle Whip

Steps:

Cook macaroni according to box instructions. Hard-boil eggs and dice. Drain peas and combine with macaroni, eggs, and tuna. Add milk, relish and mayonnaise or Miracle Whip. Mix well and puree thoroughly until a smooth consistency.

ANGEL HAIR PASTA WITH MIXED VEGETABLES AND ROASTED RED PEPPER

½ box angel hair pasta
1 can mixed vegetables
1 can red kidney beans
3 large roasted red peppers
½ *Thick & Easy* or *Resource* nectar milk

Steps:

Prepare angel hair according to instructions on the box. Add mixed vegetables and kidney beans. Add milk. Dice and add red peppers. Mix well. Place entire mixture in a food processor and puree thoroughly until smooth.

ANGEL HAIR WITH PARMESAN BROCCOLI

1 box angel hair pasta
3 eggs
1 bag frozen broccoli florets
5 handfuls Parmesan cheese
½ Thick & Easy or Resource nectar milk

Steps:

Prepare angel hair according to instructions on the box. Boil and mash broccoli. Beat 3 eggs until frothy. Microwave 2-3 minute. Combine cooked angel hair, mashed broccoli, and eggs. Add milk and Parmesan cheese. Place entire mixture in a food processor and puree thoroughly until smooth consistency.

SIMPLE SPAGHETTI

½ box angel hair pasta
2 cans diced tomatoes
1 can garbanzo beans
3 pinches of sugar
1 squirt of ketchup
½ Thick & Easy or Resource nectar milk
3 handfuls of Mozzarella cheese
3 handfuls of Parmesan cheese

Steps:

Prepare angel hair according to instructions on the box. Add diced tomatoes, garbanzo beans, sugar, ketchup, Mozzarella and Parmesan cheese. Add milk. Mix well. Place entire mixture in a food processor and puree until smooth.

FISH

TUNA WITH STUFFING

1 can Albacore Solid White tuna
1 box plain stuffing mix
1 can diced tomatoes
1 dollop onion dip
2 handfuls frozen chopped spinach
1 large red roasted pepper
3 shakes of sage
3 shakes of parsley
1 vanilla <u>Boost</u> or <u>Ensure</u>
1 egg

Steps:

Combine tuna with diced tomatoes. Add onion dip. Microwave spinach in a covered dish 3-4 minutes until soft. Beat egg until frothy. Microwave beaten egg 1 minute and add to spinach, tuna with onion dip, and tomatoes. Combine stuffing and <u>Boost</u> or <u>Ensure</u>. Mix well. Dice red pepper and add to stuffing mixture. Place all ingredients into a baking dish. Mix well and microwave 8-10 minutes until bubbly. Place into a food processor and puree until smooth.

TUNA EGG SALAD

1 can Albacore Solid White tuna
4 eggs
1 dollop onion dip
3 drizzles mayonnaise or Miracle Whip
1 can French style green beans

Steps:

Combine tuna with green beans. Beat eggs until frothy. Microwave beaten eggs 2-3 minutes until cooked. Combine tuna and green beans with onions dip and eggs. Mix well and add mayonnaise or Miracle Whip. Place in a food processor and puree until smooth.

TUNA, TOMATO, AND PEAS

1 can Albacore Solid White Tuna
1 egg
1 can diced tomatoes
1 can baby peas
4 slices potato bread
3 slices American cheese
2 handfuls Cheddar cheese
½ Thick & Easy or Resource nectar milk

Steps:

Combine tuna with tomatoes, peas and egg. Dice potato bread and soak in milk. Add to tuna mixture. Add American and cheddar cheese. Place in a baking dish and microwave 8-10 minutes until bubbly. Puree throughly in a food processor until smooth.

CRABMEAT MUSHROOM

1 package imitation crabmeat
1 can cream of mushroom soup
3 eggs
1 large roasted red pepper
1 dollop onion dip
3 handfuls shredded Cheddar cheese
2 dashes paprika
2 dashes pepper
2 splashes Worcestershire sauce

Steps:

Combine crabmeat and mushroom soup. Add onion dip to crabmeat and mushroom soup. Dice red pepper. Add red pepper, cheese, paprika, pepper, and Worcestershire. Microwave 8-10 minutes, until bubbly. Puree in a food processor until smooth.

CRABMEAT LIME

2 potatoes
1 dollop onion dip
3 handfuls mushrooms
1 container lime yogurt
1 package imitation crabmeat
5 splashes lime juice

Steps:

Dice potatoes and mushrooms. Saute together until brown. Mash together. Add crabmeat. Continue to saute' to slightly brown the crabmeat. Add lime yogurt and lime juice. Mix well and heat thoroughly. Puree in a food processor until smooth.

SEAFOOD CHEESY MUSHROOM COMBO

1 package imitation crabmeat or lobster
1 can cream of shrimp soup
1 scoop onion dip
1 can diced mushrooms
1 _Thick & Easy_ or _Resource_ nectar milk
3 eggs
5 handfuls Parmesan cheese
2 squirts mustard
2 splashes Worcestershire sauce
3 dashes paprika
3 dashes pepper

Steps:

Crumble crabmeat or lobster and combine with shrimp soup, onion dip, and nectar milk. Beat eggs until frothy and add to crabmeat/ lobster mixture. Chop and saute' mushrooms. Puree mushrooms. Add pureed mushrooms, Worcestershire, Parmesan cheese, and mustard to crabmeat/lobster mixture. Mix thoroughly. Add paprika and pepper. Place in a baking dish and microwave 10-12 minutes until bubbly. Puree thoroughly in a food processor until smooth.

SOLE, SHRIMP SAUCE AND BABY PEAS

4 thin sole fillets
1 can cream of shrimp soup
½ Thick & Easy or Resource nectar milk
1 can baby peas
3 handfuls instant potato flakes
3 drizzles onion dip
3 drizzles vegetable dip
5 dashes dill

Steps:

Combine cream soup with nectar milk. Add baby peas and potato flakes. Mix well. Add onion dip and vegetable dip. Add sole fillets and dill. Microwave 6-8 minutes in a baking dish until bubbly and sole is flaky. Puree thoroughly in a food processor until smooth.

LEMON DILL SMOKED SALMON

1 pound smoked salmon
1 dollop onion dip
1 container lemon yogurt
3 splashes lemon juice
1 drizzle vegetable dip
3 dashes dill

Steps:

Combine yogurt, lemon juice, onion dip, and vegetable dip. Stir well and add salmon and dill. Microwave 6-8 minutes in a baking dish until bubbly. Puree thoroughly in a food processor until smooth.

BABY SHRIMP WITH CAULIFLOWER AND ROASTED RED PEPPER

1 bag frozen cooked baby shrimp
1 bag frozen cauliflower
1 container lemon yogurt
2 large roasted red peppers

Steps:

Boil and mash cauliflower. Add baby shrimp. Dice red pepper. Combine cauliflower, shrimp, and red pepper with lemon yogurt. Microwave 5-6 minutes, until bubbly. Puree in a food processor until smooth.

LEMON SOY SCALLOPS WITH GREEN BEANS AND PIMENTO

1 package imitation crabmeat or lobster
1 can cream of shrimp soup
1 scoop onion dip
1 can diced mushrooms
1 _Thick & Easy_ or _Resource_ nectar milk
3 eggs
5 handfuls Parmesan cheese
2 squirts mustard
2 splashes Worcestershire sauce
3 dashes paprika
3 dashes pepper

Steps:

Dust scallops in flour and chop garlic into fine pieces. Lightly brown scallops in olive oil and garlic for 3 minutes on each side. Combine scallops with green beans, mixed vegetables and pimentos. Add yogurt and soy sauce. Mix well. Place in a baking dish and microwave 5-8 minutes, until bubbly. Puree in a food processor until smooth.

TARRAGON HALIBUT WITH BROCCOLI, TOMATO, COTTAGE CHEESE, PARMESAN AND BASIL

1 pound halibut
2 cans Thick & Easy or Resource nectar milk
5 splashes of tarragon
1 bag frozen broccoli florets
1 can diced tomatoes
1 container cottage cheese with chives
1 pinch basil
1 handful Parmesan cheese
6 Ritz crackers

Steps:

Cube halibut. Add halibut to Thick & Easy or Resource nectar milk. Microwave for 8-10 minutes, until halibut is flaky with a fork. Splash halibut and milk with tarragon. Boil and mash broccoli florets. Combine halibut and mashed broccoli. Add tomatoes, cottage cheese, basil, Parmesan cheese. Crumble Ritz crackers and add to halibut, vegetable, and cheese mixture. Soak to soften crackers. Place in a baking dish and microwave 8-10 minutes until bubbly. Puree in a food processor until smooth.

DESSERT

CINNAMON GRAHAM CANNOLI

1 small container ricotta cheese
2 scoops powdered sugar
6 squirts Hershey chocolate syrup
5 crumbled cinnamon graham crackers
1 can <u>Thick & Easy</u> or <u>Resource</u> nectar milk

Steps:

Place graham crackers into food processor and pulse until very fine. Combine ricotta cheese and sugar. Swirl sweetened cheese with Hershey chocolate syrup. Stir in nectar milk. Add graham crackers and soak until soft. Mix well. Puree in a food processor until smooth.

PUMPKIN SOUFFLE'

1 can pumpkin pie filling
1 can <u>Thick & Easy</u> or <u>Resource</u> nectar milk
3 eggs
4 shakes cinnamon
4 shakes nutmeg
1 tablespoon maple syrup
6 slices potato bread

Steps:

Beat eggs until fluffy. Stir in pumpkin pie filling, and maple syrup. Cube potato bread and soak in nectar milk. Add nutmeg and cinnamon. Mix egg mixture into soaked bread and milk. Place in a baking dish and microwave 10-12 minutes until puffy. Puree thoroughly in a food processor until smooth.

CARAMELIZED CHEESECAKE

1 package softened cream cheese
4 eggs
½ cup sugar
1 can Thick & Easy or Resource nectar milk
½ cup whole milk

Steps:

Beat eggs until fluffy. Mix together softened cream cheese and sugar. Beat eggs and sweetened cheese together. Add nectar milk and whole milk. Beat all ingredients together. Bake in a greased pan at 350 for 1½ hours. Puree in a food processor until smooth.

APPLE PIE

1 store-bought fresh baked apple pie
1 cup apple juice

Steps:

In a food processor, combine a fresh apple pie with apple juice. Puree thoroughly until smooth consistency.

As an alternative: use peach nectar for peach pie and puree and use cherry juice for cherry pie and puree with added sugar.

FRUIT PIE FILLING DESSERT

1 can cherry pie filling
1 can peach pie filling
1 can apple pie filling
1 container cherry yogurt
1 container peach yogurt
1 container apple yogurt
1 package softened cream cheese
1 egg

Steps:

Beat egg until fluffy. Add softened cream cheese. Choose flavor. For cherry: Add cherry pie filling and cherry yogurt. For peach: Add peach pie filling and peach yogurt. For apple: Add apple pie filling and apple yogurt. Mix well. In a baking dish, microwave 6-8 minutes, until bubbly. Puree thoroughly in a food processor until smooth.

CHEESY PEARS WITH LIME COCONUT

1 can sliced pears
3 dollops softened cream cheese
1 container lime yogurt
3 dollops coconut cream concentrate
2 splashes whole milk

Steps:

Combine pears and softened cream cheese. Mix well. Add yogurt and coconut cream concentrate. Microwave 3-4 minutes. Puree by adding whole milk in a food processor until smooth. Chill in the refrigerator.

CHEESY CHERRY EGG CUSTARD

5 eggs
1 can Thick & Easy or Resource nectar milk
1 package softened cream cheese
1 container cherry yogurt
1 can cherry pie filling

Steps:

Beat eggs until fluffy. Combine eggs and cream cheese. Add milk and yogurt. Mix well. Add cherry yogurt and cherry pie filling. Place in a baking pan and bake at 350 for 1½ hours, until puffy. Puree in a food processor until smooth.

As an alternative, use any fruit pie filling.

PEPPERMINT CHOCOLATE PUDDING WITH WHIPPED CREAM

½ cup Hershey chocolate syrup
2 handfuls of chocolate peppermint mint patties
1 can Thick & Easy or Resource nectar milk
1 container vanilla yogurt
1 can sweetened whipped cream

Steps:

Combine chocolate syrup and peppermint mint patties with nectar milk and yogurt. Stir. Microwave for 5 minutes. Puree in food processor until smooth. Chill for 1 hour. Serve chilled and topped with sweetened whipped cream.

PEACH MELBA

1 can peach pie filling
2 dollops raspberry jam
1 container vanilla yogurt
3 dashes cinnamon
3 dashes sugar

Steps:

Puree peach pie filling with raspberry jam and vanilla yogurt. Stir in cinnamon and sugar.

OATMEAL COOKIES AND MILK

6 oatmeal cookies
1 can <u>Thick & Easy</u> or <u>Resource</u> nectar milk

Steps:

Soak cookies in nectar milk. Puree thoroughly in a food processor until smooth.

As an alternative, use any yummy cookie.

CINNAMON EGG CUSTARD

5 eggs
1 can vanilla <u>Boost</u> or <u>Ensure</u>
1 package of softened cream cheese
5 dashes cinnamon
5 dashes sugar

Steps:

Beat eggs until fluffy. Add <u>Boost</u> or <u>Ensure</u> and cream cheese. Add cinnamon and sugar. Beat mixture until smooth. In a baking pan, bake at 350 for 1 hour until puffy. Place in a food processor and puree thoroughly until smooth consistency.

As an alternative, soak 3 slices of cubed potato bread in mixture before baking and pureeing

RESURCES

Shopping List

MEATS:

Boneless chicken, ground beef, cube steak, boneless pork chops, Italian sweet sausage, deviled ham, deli meats: turkey, ham, chicken

FISH:

Imitation crabmeat or lobster, sole, halibut, scallops, smoked salmon, cooked baby shrimp

DAIRY (LOW FAT):

Yogurt: plain, vanilla, lemon, lime, orange, strawberry, peach; milk, eggs, American cheese, Swiss cheese, cheddar cheese, plain cottage cheese, pineapple cottage cheese, cream cheese, Mozzarella cheese, Parmesan cheese, _Thick & Easy_ or _Resource_ nectar milk, butter, sour cream, onion dip, vegetable dip, canned sweetened whipped cream

BREAD:

Italian, potato, whole wheat, pumpernickel, seedless rye

CEREAL:

Cornflakes, cream of rice, rice crispies

FRESH FRUIT:

Strawberries, mango, papaya

CANNED GOODS (LOW SALT):

Kidney beans, diced tomatoes, French style green beans, baby peas, asparagus, sliced beets, coconut cream concentrate, roasted red peppers, sweet potatoes, garbanzo beans, sauerkraut, mixed vegetables, creamed corn, corned beef, tuna, tomato juice, marshmallow, deviled ham

CANNED SOUPS (LOW SALT):

Creamed soup: celery, broccoli, asparagus, shrimp; vegetable, split pea, lentil

CANNED FRUITS (LITE):

Fruit cocktail, sliced peaches, sliced pears, crushed pineapple, cranberry, mandarin oranges, honey

CANNED PIE FILLING:

Apple, cherry, peach, pumpkin

JARS:

Raspberry and strawberry jam, marmalade, mayonnaise or Miracle Whip, coconut cream concentrate, ketchup, sweet pickle relish, honey, maple syrup, ranch and vinaigrette salad dressing, Heinz gravy: beef, pork, chicken; soy sauce, Worcestershire sauce, Hershey chocolate syrup

FROZEN VEGETABLES AND FRUIT BAGS:

Spinach, broccoli florets, cauliflower, mixed vegetables, strawberries, baby peas, creamed onion, sweet potato

FRESH VEGETABLES AND FRUITS:

Summer squash, yellow squash, baby carrots, mushrooms, onions, cucumber, potatoes, strawberries, lemon, lime, avocado

POTATOES:

White, red, sweet potato, instant potato flakes

SPICES:

Pepper, basil, tarragon, ginger, dill, cinnamon, nutmeg, lemon, lime, mint jelly, curry powder, Mrs. Dash

BOXED FOODS:

Elbow macaroni, pre-cooked lasagna sheets, brown rice, graham crackers, Ritz crackers, oatmeal cookies, plain stuffing mix, chocolate peppermint mint patties, bread crumbs, white and brown sugar

STORE PREPARED FOODS:

Baked chicken, fresh apple or peach pie

THICKENED LIQUIDS:

Thick & Easy or *Resource* nectar: milk, water, cranberry juice, apple juice, *Boost* or *Ensure*: strawberry, vanilla, chocolate

THICKENING PRODUCTS:

Thick & Easy or *Resource* instant thickening powder

NUTRIENT SUPPLEMENTS:

Benecalorie, Beneprotein, Pedialyte

SOUP BASE: (LOW SALT)

Orrington Farms: beef, chicken, pork

HELPFUL INFORMATION
WHERE TO BUY PRODUCTS

Thick & Easy products are produced by Hormel Health Labs: www.hormelhealthlabs.com
Hormel Health Labs products are available for home use.

CVS.com offers a variety of shelf stable products from Hormel Health Labs. For a complete list of available products, contact CVS.com:
    PHONE: 888 607 4CVS (4287)
    http://www.CVS.com/hormel

Food processors, blenders, *NutriBullet* can be purchased at most store that have kitchen supplies:
- Bed Bath and Beyond
    www.bedbathandbeyond.com
- Sears
    www.sears.com
- Macy's
    www.macy's.com
- Walmart
    www.walmart.com

Resource products, *Benecalorie* and *Beneprotein* are produced by Novartis Medical Nutrition Labs: www.novartis.com

Novartis products can be ordered through most pharmacies.

Information about Novartis Medical Nutrition Labs and Novartis products can be found on their website: www.novartisnutrition.com/us/home

Pedialyte, Boost, and *Ensure* beverages can be purchased at most grocery stores and pharmacies.

BIBLIOGRAPHY

The Dysphagia Diet
http://www.dysphagia-diet.com

Lippincott Nursing Center
www.lippincottnursingcenter.com

Dysphagia Research Society
www.dysphagiaresearch.org

Hormel Health Labs
www.hormelheathlabs.com

National Center for BioTechnology
www.ncbi.nlm.nih.gov

Nestle Health Science
https://www.nestlehealthscience.com

The Dysphagia Institute at Froedtert & the Medical College of Wisconsin
www.froedtert.com
www.froedtert.com/gastroenterology

University of Pittsburgh Schools of the Health Sciences; University of Pittsburgh Medical Center; UPMC Swallowing Disorders Center
www.upmc.com

The Mayo Clinic
www.mayoclinic.org

Memorial Sloan Kettering Cancer Center
www.mskcc.org

The American Speech Language Hearing Association ASHA
www.asha.org

The Myositis Association
www.myositis.org

The Stroke Association
www.strokeassociation.org

The Voice And Swallowing Institute; New York Eye And Ear Infirmary of Mount Sinai
www.nyee.edu

Web MD
www.webmd.com

Medicine Net
www.medicinenet.com

Merck Manuals
www.merckmanuals.com

Cedars-Sinai Medical Center
www.cedars-sinai.edu

Roswell Park Cancer Institute
www.roswellpark.org

HOPEFULLY
THESE
SIMPLE
SAFE AND EASY
PUREE
RECIPES
ENHANCE YOUR
DYSPHAGIA-RELATED LIFESTYLE
AT
MEALTIME

66136114R00065

Made in the USA
Lexington, KY
04 August 2017